FIRST EDITION

ORGANIZE
YOURSELF HEALTHY

Mind - Time - Home - Social Life - Meal Plan - Exercise

**A PRACTICAL METHOD
TO A BALANCED LIFE
FOR BUSY MOMS**

Set clear goals - Create schedules and routines - Care for your body and soul
Master meal planning - Purge and organize your home - Exercise regularly

FEATURES

Organize your Mind

Organize your Social Life

Organize your Time

Organize your Eating Habits

Organize your Home

Organize your Health

Hello fellow moms,

I am Di Ter Avest, a Professional Home and Lifestyle Organizer, founder of Di is Organized and creator of the Organize Yourself Healthy method. Since 2013, I have helped hundreds of women rethink their relationship with stuff. Our in-person services, virtual projects, accountability programs, and workshops help women create sustainable organizational systems for their homes and lives.

As a mother of two young children, I understand:

- The struggles to keep the house clean and organized while still working a full-time job;

- How frustrating it is walking around the house when kids' toys and stuff have taken over;

- That carving time to focus on yourself while juggling work, housework, extracurricular activities, and social lives seems almost impossible.

I'll tell you one thing: I do not want to spend my days cleaning. I want every minute of my free time to be spent enjoying my family, friends, and favorite activities without guilt. Having a plan and being organized helps me achieve these goals.

We all know that real life is messy and unpredictable, and there is no one-size-fits-all approach to organizing a home and everyday tasks. Everyone is different, but organizing my mind, time, and home makes my day-to-day routine not feel like a burden to me. Having a plan makes it easier for me to create time to take care of myself, exercise, plan, and make healthy meals for the whole family.

I am an immigrant who has transformed her passion for an organized home into a business. Growing up in Brazil, I would clip articles about homemaking and lifestyle from old home magazines just because I loved reading and collecting them in a binder. At a very young age, I learned from my mother how to take care of the home and organize all of our rooms. My father was an entrepreneur himself, always teaching me about home management and budgeting without realizing it. Today, I live in Baltimore, MD, and I am a proud mom to two young kids and a wife to a great husband. I am passionate about having an organized home and life that allows me to spend quality time with the people I love.

I understand that living a healthy lifestyle isn't always easy. In fact, despite our good intentions, many situations can come up and leave us feeling that we have failed. Raise your hand if you can't remember the last time you had time for one of the activities below:

- Relaxed or dedicated time to a self-care routine
- Gotten your nails done or enjoyed other pampering
- Had a girls' night with friends
- Exercised
- Deeply connected with your spouse on a date
- Planned meals in advance
- Felt confident about yourself

I could list many other things we put aside, even though they are essential to our physical, emotional, and mental well-being. As a working mother of two young children, I understand the challenges women face as they try to achieve balance in their lives. In the past, I have even felt guilty for focusing on myself and my desires for a few minutes a day or per week.

Yet, having a healthy and organized lifestyle helps us stay focused, be present in the moment, and reduce stress. Over the years, many of my clients have asked me to help them create a plan to organize all aspects of their lives, not just their homes but also their time, meals, self-care, and social lives. With that in mind, I decided to create the Organize Yourself Healthy method to help more moms, just like us, to create a healthier, happier, and more intentional life by simply getting organized.

The Organize Yourself Healthy method will enable you to identify and eliminate time and energy drains so that you can focus on the things that matter. The Organize Yourself Healthy method will guide you through the process of how to:

- Set clear goals for yourself and map out a strategy to achieve them.
- Create a schedule that ensures you have time to care for your body and soul.
- Organize your home, making cooking healthy meals and exercising regularly easier.
- Create a plan to spend consistent and meaningful time with family and friends and build a support system to help you stick to your healthy lifestyle.
- Master your meal planning skills to keep you and your family eating well and avoid the dreaded drive-thru.
- Organize your workout routine so that you can commit to a realistic exercise schedule.

Let's customize new systems for your lifestyle to keep you moving toward your goals, even during hectic times. Take your time implementing the Organize Yourself Healthy method; you want to stick to the process and make it a habit. Spend some time following the process and creating routines to improve every facet of your life.

Success has a different meaning for each person, so you will start by identifying what a joyful, balanced life would look like for you. Define your version of healthy. What makes you happy? What goals will you set for yourself?

ORGANIZE
your mind

UNDERSTANDING YOUR MIND

When you think about human progress, you will notice that people had plenty of time for quiet contemplation not long ago (before TV and the Internet). Now, people find themselves overwhelmed with the amount of information they consume daily. The reality is that too much information can harm your mental health.

How much information do you consume on a regular day? Some information is essential for our careers, hobbies, and civic engagement. But many of us find that we take in more information than we could possibly process. We're trying to drink from a fire hose when a glass of water would be just fine. This unnecessary information competes for attention with things that really do matter to our lives.

We live in a time where many people like to multi-task; however, our brains can only focus on two or three things at a time.

Picture this scenario: after a busy day of work, you are late to pick up the kids at school. While you are getting out of the car, you see your friend and engage in a conversation right away on the way to the door. The kids are excited to tell you all about their day, and perhaps they are throwing a tantrum because they are hungry.

You try to keep the conversation going with your friend a little longer while still watching the kids. Suddenly, it starts to rain. You run to the car with the kids and realize you have no idea where you put your keys. There was too much going on in a short period of time for you to keep track of everything.

Multi-tasking can be dangerous sometimes. An overload of information and actions can overwhelm your brain and make you forget simple things that are important to you. But it is possible to reclaim a peaceful, orderly mind. Work through the Organize Yourself Healthy method steps to help you focus on one task at a time, limit the amount of information you are exposed to and create systems to organize your thoughts.

Are you familiar with the concept of "mental load"? While men today are much more engaged in their homes and families than their fathers and grandfather's generations, women often wind up being in charge of the domestic sphere while juggling professional and other responsibilities. Women often wind up being the ones who remember which groceries are needed, when the fifth grader's book report is due, when the third grader has soccer practice, when the kids go to the dentist, and when the dog goes to the groomer.

The list goes on and on. When we look around our house, we see a series of endlessly linked tasks. A man might do the dishes and leave the sink and sponge still dirty on the counter. His mission and goal were to do the dishes, not to clean the kitchen.

On the other hand, a woman would probably do the dishes, wipe down the countertops, and take the trash out because they think of cleaning holistically.

During my many years working with clients in their homes, I noticed that their cluttered spaces often result from a busy and stressful lifestyle. An organized mind is related to an organized space, and the opposite is also true. When you categorize your thoughts, you optimize your time to focus on what matters most: your health and well-being.

SET YOUR PRIORITIES

Setting priorities is key to being organized. When you understand where you are heading and what you want for your life, the rest falls into place. When you have a clear vision of your priorities, you are more likely to design your life and routines in a way that makes it easier to be healthy.

Many people struggle to figure out where to start. Some don't have a clear idea of their top priorities in life. For example, my top three priorities are family, myself, and business. In these three categories, I have events, activities, and ideas that are more important than others. I have a clear picture of which hobbies, vacations, activities, or even career activities might serve a higher purpose.

Having those priorities clear in your mind helps you make quicker and better decisions on what activity, event, or plans you will say yes to. Your priorities will guide your lifestyle and choices.

Understanding your priorities will also help you manage your time better. You will feel better when you have to say no to someone or an activity that doesn't align with your core values at that time in life.

It doesn't mean that someone or something has less value to you. It just means that at that time, you have other priorities.

Here's an example: your boss and friends from work are meeting for a happy hour on Friday after work. At the same time, your son has an event at school and expects you to be there. If you have a clear idea of your priorities, you will be able to make a quick decision without feeling guilty.

Keep in mind that your priorities can and will change from time to time, or even weekly. Everything in life needs balance. Your priorities can shift on a daily basis.

Today, for example, I am writing this part of the Organize Yourself Healthy method, and my family will need to wait a couple of hours for my attention. On Saturdays and Sundays, my priority shifts to my family and myself. On Sunday afternoons, my priority is to take care of the house and meal prep.

Now, it is your time to set your priorities. What is important to you?

NAME YOUR PRIORITIES

Once you have written down your priorities, list specific goals for each category: have a date with your spouse once a month, meal plan weekly, take the kids on an adventure every week, exercise three times a week, screen-free night once a week, etc.

SELF-CARE

FAMILY

CAREER

FINANCES

PHYSICAL +
MENTAL HEALTH

SOCIAL +
COMMUNITY

SPIRITUALITY

OTHER

MANAGING STRESS

One of the ways that our plans for ourselves get derailed is when things get stressful. As a mom, it is easy to feel like you experience every kind of stress.

Remember that our mind controls our body and emotions. You can't change the things that happen in your life — you can't predict that sudden snow day or the outbreak of hand, foot, and mouth (or COVID-19) — but you can change your reaction to it.

If you are going through a stressful moment in your life, try some new ways to calm down your mind. You could get outside, take a calming walk, call your best friend, or reframe your negative thoughts to look for the silver linings.

Create a list with some ideas to de-stress and refer to your list any time your brain is close to a shutdown.

Managing Stress List

Our mind controls our body, emotions, and how we feel about our surrounding environment. If you are going through a stressful moment, try new ways to calm your mind.

☐ Get outside

☐ Write it all down

☐ Talk to someone

☐ Distract your mind

☐ Breath Slowly

☐ Do a guided meditation

☐ Reframe negative thoughts

☐ Take a warm shower

☐ Listen to a podcast

☐ Try a new workout

☐ Believe you are a strong woman, and act like one!

WRITE YOUR AFFIRMATIONS

Henry Ford once said, "Whether you think you can or you can't, you are right." That sums up my thoughts on this subject.

From a very young age, I remember my mom telling my brothers and me how her words affected her children. She carefully chose her words so that they would empower us instead of damaging our self-images.

Our words and thoughts have a significant impact on our lives. Change your thoughts, and you will change yourself. Try not to criticize yourself too much. Treat yourself with the patience, enthusiasm, and compassion you would show a friend.

Write down affirmations that you will be able to look back on during tough times. Also, refer to them every morning while you get ready for the day. You can write them on paper, in your journal, or create a poster to hang in your closet, behind the door, or in your office. Ask your close friends, kids, and partner to write a paragraph or two that will remind you of the wonderful person you are and the hard work you do.

SETTING AFFIRMATIONS

SELF-CARE

FAMILY

CAREER

FINANCES

PHYSICAL +
MENTAL HEALTH

SOCIAL +
COMMUNITY

SPIRITUALITY

OTHER

CHARTING YOUR COURSE

Simply setting an intention is the first step to making a change. When you decide to sleep better, get more exercise, or organize your home, you will start to see things fall into place.

As you work through the steps of the Organize Yourself Healthy method, I have two requests for you: maintain a positive attitude and stay disciplined. You want to see positive changes in your life, and I want to help you get there.

Often, when we start a new routine, a new workout, a new season, or a new year, we are highly motivated. But, in time, real life creeps in, and we lose some of that enthusiasm or motivation. Well, this time, things will be different. You're going to break up these changes step by step, creating new habits in a timely and manageable way.

I'd like you to think about your expectations and goals. What are the changes you are looking to make? Be honest with yourself. Take some time to think and write down your thoughts. After you write down your vision for your future, set some small and manageable goals.

Here are some examples:

- If you want to exercise more often, set a specific goal of how often you would like to work out and for how long.

- Perhaps your goal is to spend more time with your family. When would you be able to carve some time? Will you need to block a day or time?

- Or, if your goal is to eat healthier food, elaborate on what foods you would like to have, where you will buy them, and when you can prepare them.

Don't be afraid of starting small and becoming more ambitious as you go. Take one small step after another. Build momentum and give yourself room to grow. If you haven't exercised in a long time, don't plan to suddenly start working out every day. Set manageable goals, like going to the gym two or three times a week.

If you are a perfectionist like me, you might feel scared of changing your habits and worry you might mess up. But I'm here to tell you that you can improve your life. I know it because I have done it myself. Believe in yourself and your power to shape your destiny!

SETTING GOALS

Remember, be specific and realistic

SELF-CARE

FAMILY

CAREER

FINANCES

PHYSICAL +
MENTAL HEALTH

SOCIAL +
COMMUNITY

SPIRITUALITY

OTHER

START A JOURNAL

Have you ever thought about journaling? I used to do it when I was a girl but forgot about it for a long time. A couple of years ago, after I had kids, I started journaling again because I wanted to remember the details of their childhoods.

Journals are an excellent place to write about our mental health, organization, routines, mood, affirmations, goals, and much more.

To me, the appearance of a journal doesn't matter. What does matter is that it invites you to write and explore your thoughts. Journaling helps you work through problems, achieve goals, become more mindful, stay organized, reduce stress levels, practice gratitude, and much more.

Don't know where to start? There are many options out there. There are digital and paper journals, such as notebooks, planners, and sketchbooks. The most important thing is the journal will work for your purposes.

When it comes to writing, you can feel free write all the things in your mind until you are done. I actually use my journal to make lists, plans, re-evaluate my goals, do brain dumps, and brainstorm about my life and goals. You bet I wrote about the Organize Yourself Healthy method in my journal months, if not years ago. Like everything else we have discussed so far, there's no "right" or "wrong" way of doing it. Use your journal the way that works best for you.

THE HIGHLIGHTS OF MY DAY

DATE

WHAT MADE ME HAPPY TODAY? WHAT AM I THANKFUL FOR?

ORGANIZE
your time

"YOU'RE WRITING THE STORY OF YOUR LIFE ONE MOMENT AT A TIME"

- Doc Childre and Howard Martin -.

UNDERSTANDING HOW YOU USE YOUR TIME

It is time to focus on arranging your time to accomplish your goals. With the hard work you are investing in this, you will create a healthier, happier, and more intentional life.

Evaluate where you are spending your time and how to direct it to the things you actually want to do.

Before you start organizing your time, track how you use your time for an entire day. Keep this diary with you throughout the day and try to fill it out in the moment. That way, you will have a much more accurate portrait of how you spend your time. It's important to write down these notes in real-time. When we try to remember how we spent our time, we skip over the time spent sitting in traffic, chatting with co-workers, or scrolling through social media. A time diary provides real insight into your time, minute-by-minute. This exercise is an essential step to observe how you have been spending your time and where you need to improve.

Time Diary

How do you use your time right now? Track your day to realize how you have been spending your time and where you need to improve.

TIME	ACTIVITY	TIME	ACTIVITY
5:30		10:45	
5:45		11:00	
6:00		11:15	
6:15		11:30	
6:30		11:45	
6:45		12:00	
7:00		12:15	
7:15		12:30	
7:30		12:45	
7:45		1:00	
8:00		1:15	
8:15		1:30	
8:30		1:45	
8:45		2:00	
9:00		2:15	
9:15		2:30	
9:30		2:45	
9:45		3:00	
10:00		3:15	
10:15		3:30	
10:30		3:45	

TIME	ACTIVITY	TIME	ACTIVITY
4:00		9:15	
4:15		9:30	
4:30		9:45	
4:45		10:00	
5:00		10:15	
5:15		10:30	
5:30		10:45	
5:45		11:00	
6:00		11:15	
6:15		11:30	
6:30		11:45	
6:45		12:00	
7:00			
7:15			
7:30			
7:45			
8:00			
8:15			
8:30			
8:45			
9:00			

USE YOUR TIME WISELY

I love a quote by Charles Buxton: "You will never find time for anything. If you want time, you must make it." That is what we are here to do — make time for the things that are important to you.

Do you often wonder at the end of the day where all your time went? Time seems just to disappear when we don't sit down and put some effort into organizing it. When you organize your time, you can live more in the moment instead of stressing out about all you have to do. To me, it is all about quality versus quantity.

Today is your chance to take control of time instead of letting it take control of you. After these exercises, you will be shocked to see how much time you actually have and how much better you feel when you put it to good use

Here are some questions to guide your thoughts and help you determine where to improve.

- What are the things you don't enjoy doing but have to do every day?

- What are the activities you think are wasting your time each day?

- What tasks would you love to remove from your life?

- What could you outsource?

Now, it is time to daydream a little bit. Think about what your ideal day would look like. I don't mean your perfect day on vacation, but the perfect day right now, with all work, family, and relationship obligations. How can you structure your time to meet your goals best? What activities must happen daily for you to live as you would like? Remember that you are in charge of designing your own happiness and success. Don't worry about what other people would think or do. You are creating your version of a good life.

As an example, my perfect day includes the following activities:

- Exercise (15-30 min)

- Eat healthy and simple meals

- Pray/meditate/and say my affirmations (15min)

- 4-6 hours of work with clients and/or on the business

- Play with my kids (no electronics - 30 min to 1 hour)

- Eat at least one meal each day as a family

- Some non-distracted time with my husband

- A little bit of self-care

- 6-8 hours of sleep

It doesn't matter what time most of these things happen in my day. It is rare when two days are precisely the same due to our many obligations.

Some of you might be thinking that all these things I am sharing here might be easier said than done. Yes, you could be correct, but it is entirely up to you to put in the effort to move closer to your goals. I guarantee you can create a better, healthier, and more organized future. All you have to do is replace your bad habits with good ones to become the person you want to be.

Be honest with yourself! You set the course of your life. You have the power to change how you spend your time, your days, and your life.

Do not procrastinate. Some activities and routines you don't even notice might be making you waste your precious time. Identify yours and learn how to avoid black holes that suck up your time, especially the phone and the TV.

For example, I used to love watching Brazilian soap operas. One summer, I went to Brazil to visit my family and ended up getting sucked into the drama of a soap opera, and I couldn't let it go when we came back. I asked my brother to sign up for the online channel since I can't buy it here in the US, so I could keep watching the drama. The problem is that the episodes are one hour long and air Monday through Saturday. That added up to 6 hours of my week that I could be doing something more productive, but "thanks to my addiction," I was not. I have no idea how people in Brazil get anything done in their evenings.

Soap operas start at 5:30 p.m., and there are four of them, back to back, until 9:30 p.m. I was so glad when the soap opera I was watching was over because I got that time back to do more productive things.

So, as you know now, my weaknesses are soap operas and other TV shows. What are yours? TV, phone, social media, games? Naming your distractions will help you regain that time and put it to good use.

Turn off notifications on your phone and designate specific times throughout the day to check your email or social media. Use these activities as rewards for yourself, just as you do for the kids.

TIME MANAGEMENT

Write down the things you don't enjoy doing but have to do every day, the activities you think are wasting your time, activities you would love to outsource, etc.

....

....

....

....

....

....

MY IDEAL DAILY ACTIVITIES

MORNING

AFTERNOON

EVENING

CREATE A MASTER TO-DO LIST

I love checking off completed tasks on a piece of paper. It is so satisfying, isn't it?
Remember the brain-dump exercise you did to get everything out of your mind into the paper? Now it is time
to write down all the things you want, plan, and have to do on a piece of paper. You will spend some time
adding items until you can't think of anything else. Even those house updates you have been putting off for
years can go on this list. You can categorize your to-do list if it gets too long.

- [ ] _____
- [ ] _____
- [ ] _____
- [ ] _____
- [ ] _____
- [ ] _____
- [ ] _____
- [ ] _____
- [ ] _____
- [ ] _____
- [ ] _____
- [ ] _____
- [ ] _____
- [ ] _____
- [ ] _____

CATEGORIZED TO-DO LIST

Category 1: _ _ _ _ _ _ _ _ _ _ _ _ _ _ _ _

Category 2:_ _ _ _ _ _ _ _ _ _ _ _ _ _ _ _ _

Category 3:_ _ _ _ _ _ _ _ _ _ _ _ _ _ _ _

Category 4: _ _ _ _ _ _ _ _ _ _ _ _ _ _ _ _

Category 5: _ _ _ _ _ _ _ _ _ _ _ _ _ _

Category 6:_ _ _ _ _ _ _ _ _ _ _ _ _ _

Category 7:_ _ _ _ _ _ _ _ _ _ _ _ _ _

Category 8: _ _ _ _ _ _ _ _ _ _ _ _ _ _

CREATE AN EVENING ROUTINE

Did you know that a successful day starts the night before? You set yourself up for success when you get everything in order in the evening. Establishing an evening routine that keeps you worry-free and well-rested can make all the difference.

Your evening routine could include:

- Tidying up the house
- Sweeping the floor in the most used areas
- Loading and running the dishwasher
- Instructing the kids to clean up the toys (even toddlers can learn how to clean up after themselves)
- Selecting clothes for the next day
- Pre-packing lunches

- Setting up the coffee machine
- Checking what is on the schedule for the next day
- Creating a to-do list for the next day
self-care (yoga, meditation, journaling, reading)

What could you do for an hour or so before going to bed to ensure your day will start on a better note the following day?

To give you another example of how a routine can set up the mood for your night and day, I will share our experience with our kids. Since the first day we returned from the hospital with our babies, we implemented a bedtime routine for them. Every night, at 7 p.m., we bathed them, put pajamas on, and read books. Then the lights go out. This routine helped them know — even when they were tiny — what was coming and the difference between night and day. Every night they knew what to expect. Fast forward seven years, and both children still have the same routine!

A couple of things got added with time. For example, they know they need to tidy up (primarily toys and electronics) before they can have some screen time.

An evening routine will help even if one of your goals is losing weight. Did you know that people who stay up late consume more calories than those who go to sleep at reasonable and predictable hours each night? An organized and consistent schedule won't just make you feel better but will keep you focused and help you reach your goals.

INITIATE A MORNING ROUTINE

The positive or negative actions in the first hours of your day can determine your day. That is why it is crucial to have an evening routine. That helps you to set up a good mood in the morning.

Tell me which scenario you like best:

A) You wake up about one hour before everybody else. Your workout clothes are already there, waiting for you by the side of your bed. You do your daily dose of exercise, take a shower and get ready! You go to the kitchen; everything is peaceful and in its place. The kitchen is clean and ready for you to prepare a delicious and nutritious breakfast.

or

B) You wake up, and before you even leave your room to go to the bathroom, you trip on something on the floor. The bathroom is a mess with all the bath toys and clothes from bath time the night before. You keep moving and make your way to the kitchen. On the way, you pass by the living room and step on a Lego. In the kitchen, you see the mountain of dishes to be done; they are everywhere, making it almost impossible to make a cup of coffee.

Which scenario would you pick?

Wouldn't it be better if you had a friendly, peaceful environment welcoming you in the morning? You can find the time to care for yourself before you start caring for everything and everybody else.

Here are some ideas of what your morning routine could look like.

- Wake up before other family members
- Workout for about 30 minutes
- Meditate on your day and your affirmations
- Shower
- Get ready, head to toe
- Have breakfast with the family
- Get kids ready for school
- Take kids to school
- Go to work

You can add as much or as little to your morning routine. Take everything into consideration: where you exercise, how the kids behave in the morning, if you need to be at work at a specific time, etc. Think about what fits the time you have and what would make you happy.

MY POWERFUL ROUTINE

MORNING

- [ ]
- [ ]
- [ ]
- [ ]
- [ ]
- [ ]
- [ ]
- [ ]

EVENING

- [ ]
- [ ]
- [ ]
- [ ]
- [ ]
- [ ]
- [ ]
- [ ]

PLAN YOUR WEEK / MONTH

Now that your evening and morning routines are mapped out do the same for your week and month.

Some activities and chores don't need daily updates, which is totally okay. For example, you don't need to tidy up the fridge daily or go grocery shopping weekly if you don't want to. Other activities are better done on a particular day of the week or month.

Please take a minute to think of them before writing them down on their respective spot.

Here are some ideas of what your morning routine could look like.

- Date night
- Grocery shopping
- A particular fitness class
- Prep food

Your monthly routine could also include:

- Deep cleaning a specific area of the house
- Girls night out
- Clean out the purse
- Pick a new book

Now, it is time for you to work on your lists.

MONTHLY ROUTINES

JANUARY	FEBRUARY	MARCH

JULY	AUGUST	SEPTEMBER

APRIL	MAY	JUNE

OCTOBER	NOVEMBER	DECEMBER

WEEKLY ROUTINES

SUNDAY

MONDAY

TUESDAY

WEDNESDAY

THURSDAY

FRIDAY

SATURDAY

MAKE TIME FOR SELF-CARE

I can guarantee that everything will fit your schedule, and you will achieve a healthier, happier, and more intentional life in no time. All you have to do is to get organized and be determined. Before you get to the final planning of your weekly schedule, I want to remind you of an important step: self-care!

When you start writing down your weekly schedule, start by adding some self-care and other priorities in your life. The chances are that if you don't schedule them, they will never happen.

Treat these appointments with yourself as you would treat a fun evening with your best friend. Would you promise your friend you would meet with her and then change the plan at the last minute to just stay on the couch watching TV or scrolling through social media? I bet not! Do the same when you schedule your moments to recharge, exercise, or do something just for you. Show up for yourself!

SELF-CARE ROUTINE IDEAS

Which activities make you feel happy, healthy, and confident? Write down the activities you will implement to your lifestyle and how often they will take place.

PHYSICAL

- Exercise
- Pampering
- Balanced diet

MENTAL

- Meditation
- Journaling
- Podcast

EMOTIONAL

- Affirmations
- Brain dump
- Saying no

GROWTH

- Socialize
- Hobbies
- Gratitude

DAILY

WEEKLY

MONTHLY

CREATING YOUR SCHEDULE

The last step in organizing your time is crafting a schedule that will enable you to set aside time to reach your goals and take part in activities that are meaningful and important to you.

- Begin with obligations that must be done on a specific day and time. For example: kids' school drop off and pick up times, meetings, classes, work, etc.

- After that, add essential activities for your health and well-being, such as workouts, date nights, a night out with friends, self-care routines, and fun activities with the kids. Things that make you happy and put a smile on your face.

- Lastly, you will block time on your schedule for house chores, meal planning, grocery shopping, budgeting, etc.

Allow enough flexibility in your schedule so that you have time to take the stairs instead of the elevator if you feel like it. Keep your schedule flexible for a walk after dinner or a game before bedtime. You didn't have time to go to the gym because the kids were around all day? Embrace the situation and take them on a bike ride, hiking, swimming, or working out at home with them.

I recommend using time blocking to create your schedule. When time blocking, you focus on one task, big or small, at a time and work on it until it is over. This method can limit distractions, and you get things done faster.

For example, I am here working on the Organize Yourself Healthy method. I blocked three hours to write a couple of steps. Next week, I will block time to work on formatting and editing. After that, I will create the graphics. This process allows me to focus on one task, finish it, and move on.

You can apply the same method to any area of your life. Let's use it for household chores since our next module is about organizing your environment. Block some time and work on one room at a time until you finish. Once you finish, you can move on to something else. This method will help prevent distractions.

Imagine this scenario: your goal is to clean and organize the primary bedroom. However, when you take something to the bathroom, you notice the dirty sink and start wiping it down. While you're doing that, you see some laundry on the floor. You go to put it in the hamper, but it is full, so you take some laundry to the laundry room and put it in to wash. On your way back, you pass through the kitchen and notice that the kids didn't put their plates in the sink; you go to do that and start tidying up the dining room. The day goes on, and you feel like you did so much but didn't accomplish anything. The problem is that you got so distracted by other tasks that you didn't complete your goal of cleaning the primary bedroom.

Now, it is time for you to make a first draft of your organized schedule. Allow some time for you to get used to it and make adjustments as needed. Do not over-schedule since you will need time to work on other areas of your life, such as home organizing, social activities, meal planning, etc.

Once you have a final schedule laid out, stick with it for a while. Keep it visible on your command center (or fridge) for quick reminders. If you are more of a tech person, you could work on the paper template and transfer it to your electronic calendar.

A consistent routine will help you develop discipline. However, allow time for spur-of-the-moment decisions to keep life fun and spontaneous. Keep in mind that there will always be situations that are out of your control. The schedule is here to guide you through your day and help you control time to the best of your ability.

It is important to have an open mind and accept that sometimes change will be necessary. If you diverge from the schedule, do not feel like a failure or lose your motivation. You can pick up from where you stopped and move on.

CREATE YOUR SCHEDULE

	SUN	MON	TUE	WED	THU	FRI	SAT
6:00							
7:00							
8:00							
9:00							
10:00							
11:00							
12:00							
1:00							
2:00							
3:00							
4:00							
5:00							
6:00							
7:00							
8:00							
9:00							
10:00							
11:00							
12:00							

ORGANIZE
your home

IT'S TIME TO DECLUTTER AND ORGANIZE

It is time to delve into the topic that I love the most — organizing your home; after all, creating tidy, harmonious living spaces is of utmost importance. The goal is to declutter your whole house, but to start, focus on your kitchen, fridge, pantry, and workout gear.

It is time to delve into the topic I love the most — organizing your home; after all, creating tidy, harmonious living spaces is of utmost importance. The goal should be for you to declutter your whole house, but I guide you to purge and organize your kitchen, fridge, pantry, and workout gear.

Before you begin, take pictures of these spaces to track your progress and be proud of your achievements. I hope you are feeling good about all you have accomplished with each exercise of the Organize Yourself Healthy method. To achieve a healthier, happier, and more intentional life, you will need to invest some time following through with each step. Let's get started!

SET YOUR GOALS AND EXPECTATIONS

Living or working in a cluttered, disorganized environment is stressful, and a cluttered space leads to a cluttered mind. Some people even relate the stress of a messy environment to emotional eating and other disorders. But it's possible to live intentionally and replace bad habits with good ones. Believe that you can become the person YOU want to be.

We have already laid the groundwork for this next step by decluttering your mind and creating routines and schedules. Remember that a messy space makes it harder to find the items you need to live your healthy life. If you can not find your workout clothes or your keys, you'll probably miss your class. If the kitchen is messy and the pantry and fridge overflowing, you'll struggle to prepare healthy meals.

Getting organized is magical! When your environment, time, mind, and relationships are orderly, you have the platform to build the life you always wanted.

Write down your goals and expectations for each room of your house by asking yourself these questions:

- What activities take place here?
- What is working in this space?
- What is not working?
- What stresses you the most in this space?
- What do you love about this space?
- How do you want this room to feel/look at the end of each day?

After you answer these questions, define your goals and expectations for the room.

SPACE PLANNING

LIVING ROOM	DINING ROOM	KITCHEN

PRIMARY BEDROOM	BEDROOM 2	BEDROOM 3

ENTRYWAY / PORCH

LAUNDRY ROOM

GARAGE

BATHROOM

PLAYROOM

OTHER

PURGE THE HOUSE

Before you start purging and decluttering, review your list of goals and expectations to define where to start and what your final destination is.

One of the most important things you can do to reach your health goals is to eliminate behaviors that are holding you back. I will give you a couple of examples.

Let's say your goal for your primary bedroom is to be a place to relax after a busy day of work, and you want it to feel like a luxurious hotel room. However, all you see are piles of paper on the floor, clothes everywhere, and dirty dishes on the nightstand. You get the picture. Start by stopping your negative behavior instead of adding anything to this room. For example, paper, work materials, and bills should not be in your bedroom. Your bedroom is a space you want to relax and destress, right? Your closet shouldn't be filled with clothes that you don't use or love. Make room for the ones you use regularly and love, and stop buying clothes impulsively. Finally, stop eating in your bedroom. That way, the dirty dishes will not pile up there.

Another example would be if your home is all organized, and your goal is to work on getting healthier. You want to get in shape (whatever that might be for you). The first thing to do is purge all that junk (delicious) food from your home.

The main idea here is to stop adding more and more to your house and life. The more things you have, the more time you will spend dealing with them. That means you have less time to do the things that matter most to you.

I am not saying you have to become a minimalist (but you can, if you want). I do not want you to give away everything you have, use, and love. I do not want you to get rid of all your holiday decorations. I am not going to set a number of items for you to throw away each day. That is just not my style! Everyone has a different lifestyle and different needs, and that is okay. You know what is best for you and your lifestyle. But please, consider purging your home! There is always stuff that should go.

This task may take longer for some than others. That is okay! Start where you are and keep moving! Set aside some days just for a deep decluttering session of the whole house.

Get five bags or boxes and label them: trash, donate, sell, fix, and find a new home. Walk through the house, and anything that fits these categories has to go. After decluttering your home, consider doing the same for your car and office space.

DECLUTTERING IDEAS

LIVING ROOM

- Magazines / Newspapers
- Games that are missing pieces
- Letters
- Outdated electronics
- Manuals
- Unused tea light candles
- Old batteries
- Old drink coasters

BEDROOM AND CLOSET

- Old makeup
- Worn-out sheets and bedding
- Old pillows
- Purses you never use
- Clothes, socks, and underwear with holes
  Clothes and accessories don't fit you, or you don't wear and love.
- Gifts you don't love
- Rusty jewelry
- Old prescription glasses and sunglasses

KIDS' ROOM

- Outgrown clothing
- Excess children's artwork
- Books

BATHROOM

- Towels
- Toiletries
- Expired or sample-sized toiletries
- Worn-out bath mats

HOME OFFICE

- Receipts
- Lanyards, name tags, etc., from conferences/meetings
- Business Cards
- Cards with no sentimental value
- Coupons you won't use
- School books you won't need again
- Planners from previous years

KITCHEN ORGANIZATION

We can do many things to care for our health, but what comes to my mind first is eating good food that nourishes the body and mind and provides the right amount of carbs, protein, fiber, etc. To create a healthy diet, you will need healthy eating habits and an organized kitchen where you can find everything you need to cook a healthy meal.

This task could be nerve-wracking for some of you but fear not. It is easier than you think.

- Start on one small area, such as the silverware drawer.

- Consider tossing or donating duplicate utensils or items you haven't used in years.

- If you lack space in your cabinets, the occasional tools you use once or twice a year can go in a clear box in the basement or garage labeled "special occasion kitchen gadgets."

- Keep kitchen items near the area you use them so you don't have to walk across the room to get what you need. For example, keep spatulas near the stove and coffee filters near the coffee maker.

- Create stations to make things easier to find, use, and put away — baking station, drink station, breakfast station, etc.

- If you lack counter space, consider emptying one area of your cabinets for small appliances that are usually on the countertop.

Now that you know what to do, go to the kitchen and start the organization process. Try not to get overwhelmed if it looks like a bomb went off in your kitchen during this process. It's normal. Things get worse before they get better.

KITCHEN AND PANTRY DECLUTTERING IDEAS

We can do many things to care for our health, but what comes to my mind first is eating good food that nourishes the body and mind and provides the right amount of carbs, protein, fiber, etc. To create a healthy diet, you will need healthy eating habits and an organized kitchen where you can find everything you need to cook a healthy meal.

EXPIRED
- Food
- Spices
- Vitamins
- Medication
- Drinks

OLD
- Party supplies
- Cleaning products
- Recipe books you don't use
- Plastic containers without a lid
- Mismatched containers

EXTRAS
- Mugs
- Glasses
- Appliances
- Cooking utensils
- Take out chopsticks.
- Fancy serving bowls

PANTRY

Now it's time to organize your pantry and stock it with healthy staples.

- Empty and wipe out shelves.
- Take measurements for necessary supplies, such as baskets, risers, canisters, etc.
- Check expiration dates and throw out any food that has gone bad.
- Unopened and unexpired food that doesn't match your diet goals can be donated to a local food pantry.
- Create zones for canned goods, dinners, snacks, kids' snacks, drinks, bulk items, nuts, dried fruit, etc.
- Label the shelves so you and everybody else in the house know where to put things back.

Now that your pantry is clutter-free and organized don't think your job is done. The pantry is one of the areas of the house that needs constant tidying. Every time you go grocery shopping, you will need to decant the food, eliminate extra packaging, restock baskets, etc. The labels will ensure that groceries are put in the right spot.

One last tip: think about your kids when planning the space. If you want the little ones to have the independence to get their snacks, store them on the bottom shelves to avoid them climbing the pantry to find what they want.

FRIDGE

When was the last time you cleaned and organized your fridge? How often do you do it? You can do a quick cleaning of the refrigerator every Friday or Saturday morning before going grocery shopping. That way, you know what we didn't consume the week before and have everything organized for the busy week ahead. Knowing what not to buy that week at the grocery store helps you spend your money wisely and reduce food waste.

The first step is to deep clean the refrigerator and freezer.

- You will need a sponge, vinegar and water, vanilla extract, bins, baskets, and liner (if available).
- Remove everything from the refrigerator and put the items on the kitchen countertop, table, or in a cooler. Remove the shelves and drawers.

- Wipe down the walls with vinegar and water.
- Wash shelves and drawers with soap and warm water.
- Put some vanilla extract on paper towels and rub the fridge walls.
- Rearrange the shelves if necessary and use liners if desired.
- Throw away expired food and condiments.
- Wipe down every jar and food container before returning it to the clean refrigerator.
- Create zones: baby food, grab-and-go snacks, sandwich fixing basket, etc.

You can repeat the same process for your freezer, check and change the water filter, and even work on any maintenance your refrigerator might need. You can repeat the deep cleaning process of the fridge at the beginning of each season or two times a year. Add these tasks to your schedule so you remember to complete them.

FOOD STORAGE GUIDE

FRIDGE
TOP SHELF
- Best for leftovers
- Dairy

TOP / MIDDLE
- Sandwich basket

BOTTOM SHELF
- Perfect for keeping meat, poultry, and fish.
- Milk
- Eggs

DRAWERS
- Keep fruit and vegetables separate
- High humidity drawer: broccoli, cauliflower, carrots, leafy greens
- Low humidity drawer: ripe avocados, peaches, apples, grapes, melon, pears, berries.

FRIDGE DOOR
- Top shelf
- Butter
- Jams

TOP / MIDDLE
- Condiments

BOTTOM SHELF
- Beverages

FREEZER
- Don't freeze bread for longer than three months.
- Keep meat on the bottom shelf.
- Create areas for vegetables, fruits, meat, and others.

WORKOUT GEAR

By now, your home should be less cluttered and your kitchen set up for success. Now, let's focus on you for a little bit. How is your workout routine going? Are you motivated enough to wake up early in the morning, put your workout clothes on, and hit the gym? Or do you have a hard time gathering what you need? If you always know where to find your gear, such as sneakers, headphones, water bottles, and athletic clothes, heading out the door for your workouts will be much easier. Even if you exercise at home, you will still be more likely to exercise if you can easily find all your stuff.

What is the best place to keep those items: your bedroom, home gym, or a packed gym bag? What would work for you?

If you go to the gym and keep everything in a bag, empty dirty clothing into the hamper and restock it with clean ones as soon as you return home. It is also a good idea to always keep a bag of toiletries in the gym bag so you are always prepared to freshen up after a workout.

If you exercise at home, you will also need a space to keep your weights, mat, and other equipment. That could mean a sturdy basket, a shelf, or even a closet, depending on how much gear you have.

During the COVID-19 pandemic, many people tried to find new ways to keep their bodies active. Some got into cycling; others transformed their garages into a gym. Consider those changes when organizing your space.

ORGANIZE
your social life

WHY ORGANIZING YOUR SOCIAL LIFE IS IMPORTANT

We are used to organizing papers, closets, and schedules. Yet many people may find the concept of organizing their social life a bit odd. They might think planning their dinners and phone calls with friends makes them less fun or spontaneous.

However, as busy mothers, we understand that finding time to share with the people we cherish can be challenging. Often, our calendars get filled with work and other obligations, and we don't spend as much time as we would like with family and friends.

It is time to get more intentional with your time and prioritize spending time with people you love. Check the following tips to get you started.

ORGANIZE YOUR ADDRESS BOOK

I am from Brazil; you might know this by now, but being so far from my family and friends for so long made me realize the power of keeping in touch with the ones I love.

In some ways, social media makes it easier to stay in touch, but people often just share the good stuff on their social media. You don't get a sense of what is really going on in their lives — their struggles and needs. You can't be present for friends to give them the help they need if you aren't communicating on a deeper level.

Phone calls, emails, snail mail, and visits can help us keep in touch with the ones we love. Creating a master address book with the personal information of your friends and family is essential. I like to keep this information on paper and electronically. You never know when you will lose your phone, lose access to your social media accounts, or misplace your address book.

It is a good idea to take note of a contact's full name, complete address, phone numbers, and birthday. This way, it will be easy to reach them whether you want to send a holiday card or wish to acknowledge their birthday.

So, think about how you will organize your address book. Will you create a paper one or an electronic version to start? If you use Gmail, you can update the information in the contact section. Other apps keep track of this data for you as well. However, don't let technology distract you from your real mission. If you have a piece of paper and a pen,

start getting that information on the paper. You can always start simple and get fancier later.

Get all this information together so keeping in touch with friends is more effortless.

ADDRESS BOOK TEMPLATE

Name:

Address:

City:

State:

Zip Code

Home Phone Number:

Cell Number:

Email:

Birthday:

Family Members:

Birthdays:

SET GOALS TO BE SOCIAL AND IMPROVE YOUR RELATIONSHIPS

What are your goals when it comes to your social life? What would make you happier? Where do you need to improve? Take your time to think through your relationships and analyze them. Start by creating four categories, but feel free to include other categories if needed. The categories are close family members (parents/siblings), partner, kids or pets, and close friends.

Please make a list of the top 10 or so people in your life and divide them into the categories. Next to their names, write down:

- Why these people are essential in your life

- How you have treated and nourished these relationships

- How much time you dedicated to them in the past week or month

Now, take some time to envision the future. What are the steps you could take to improve the relationship? Brainstorm some concrete activities, meetings, or dates you could share with these people. Never stop investing in the people who mean the most to you.

When you spend time with these special people, try to step back and talk about the things that really matter. Show how much you are interested in what they have to say. Imagine it was the last time you were going to see each other. Think about how you would leave this person. What are the things you couldn't go without telling them? What emotions and feelings would you like to express to them?

I know and understand that there are different kinds of people, and, at this point, I can't understand your situation and your relationship with people in your life. I will start these conversations and suggestions thinking everything is okay and you have a healthy relationship with the people we mention. If you need more in-depth help with a situation, speaking with a therapist or counselor is always helpful.

As much as you want to identify relationships to nourish, it is also important to identify toxic relationships. Do you have an old friend who is very negative, very critical, or unkind towards you? Consider cutting back on the time you talk to or spend with that person. Don't let them jeopardize your good intentions, self-esteem, and self-love.

PARENTS

If you are in a period in your life when you love spending time with your parents, grandparents, siblings and other relatives, make the most of these relationships. Schedule some family dinners and activities and enjoy time with the people who know you the best.

PARTNER

Living with the love of your life isn't always easy, but it's totally worth it. People are different; they have different backgrounds, tastes, opinions, and reactions. They were raised differently; they see things differently than you do. However, your partner is still the love of your life, no matter how different you are.

With time, a relationship's "honeymoon phase" wears off and we get lazy and often take it for granted. We stop appreciating all the good things. We stop investing in the relationship. Just think: when was the last magical moment you spent together, that you felt that both of you were present for each other?

The quote "Choose your love, then love your choice." by Thomas Monson is a great reminder for couples. How can you improve your relationship with your partner in the next week or month? Where can you find time in your schedule to include more date nights and quality time spent as a couple? Yes, I did say put it in your calendar. You know why? Because, until you make this a habit, you will need to schedule to ensure it happens.

KIDS

Maybe only a mom can understand the challenges other moms go through. If you have kids, you might know what I am talking about and where I want to go with this topic.

If you are anything like me, you are full of mommy guilt, head-to-toe guilt.

Friends, here are some truths we all should hear from time to time: You are amazing the way you are. You are the best mom your kid(s) could ever have. You can do whatever you put your mind and heart into. You are enough!

So, how do you still improve your relationship with your kids? Well, make time for them, just as you do for other relationships. Aim to spend some time each day connecting with each child one-on-one. That could mean talking with them on the way to school or getting down on the floor and playing LEGOs with them.

Try to schedule periodic special outings with each child, where you make special memories together. But keep in mind that what children most want is your time and attention. Put the laundry and the cleaning aside for a while, and get down to your child's level. Read a story, draw together, play a game, or just listen to them make up a story with their toys. Put aside distractions, like phone, email, and TV, and focus on your child.

And if you find yourself swamped with household chores, talk to your partner about it. Find new ways to divvy up the household work so that each of you has time to connect with the kids.

FRIENDS

Ah, friends! We love them, but sometimes life gets so busy that they are pushed to the back burner. As we grow older and get busier with work, children, spouses, and taking care of the home, it can be harder to find time to connect with friends. So, plan how to make girls' night out a reality again. Schedule at least one fun activity with your friends a month or every two months. If it's not on your calendar, it's not a priority.

THE VIP LIST

Create a master list of relationship goals, date ideas, why they are essential to you, and how you see your future together.

Name ....

Relationship ....

Goals ....

PUT TOGETHER A SUPPORT TEAM

Now that you have reconnected with the people dearest to you, or at least have planned to do so, get them to cheer on you and support your version of a healthy life.

Your friends are an integral part of your support team as you strive for a healthier life. While having your spouse and children's support is great, your friends will most likely see things from another perspective. Many women have internalized guilt for not living a perfect life, and they may hide their imperfections and isolate themselves by not even asking for help. They usually feel lonely trying to make these life changes alone.

Discuss your lifestyle goals with those close to you. The support of your community can make it easier for you to change your lifestyle and maintain your new healthier habits.

To create your support team, you will need to:

- Be open about the changes you are going through.

- Ask for help when you are overwhelmed and in need of some self-care.

- Find your online tribe for support.

- Be proud of yourself and confident. You should always be cheering on yourself and celebrating small victories every day.

As you can see, finding and putting your support team together will make a difference in your everyday life. Your very next best friend and supporter could be anywhere. Be open to new friendships and share your journey.

CALL A FRIEND DAY

Now that you have a list of the most influential people in your life, you have identified how you could improve these relationships and have a plan of what to do; it is time to put it into practice. All you have to do is pick one person from your VIP list that you haven't talked with for a long time and make a move.

Pick up the phone! Call this person to catch up or to make plans to meet in person soon.

Who will you contact first? Make this a habit by setting a date and time on your schedule to call a friend every week. Perhaps you have a day when you'll be in the car for a while. Use that time to call a friend.

You can go back to the draft of your schedule, check when you could fit these calls every week, and write them down there.

GET SOCIAL: ATTEND AN EVENT

The last suggestion I have to share with you is to get social. Go out. Meet new people, go to different places, travel, take a class for fun, and live your best life. Don't wait to live the life you dream about.

Take some time to look for social events in your area that you would like to attend virtually or in person. These events serve two purposes: a way to learn about yourself and a way to connect with others.

There are so many options out there. Look for mom's group meet-ups, entrepreneur meet-ups, book clubs, cooking classes, women's meet-ups, networking events, volunteering for a cause you support, religious small groups, etc.

What will be your first social event? Start planning today. Take note of the events you plan to attend monthly.

SOCIAL EVENTS CALENDAR

JANUARY	FEBRUARY	MARCH

APRIL	MAY	JUNE

SOCIAL EVENTS CALENDAR

JULY	AUGUST	SEPTEMBER

OCTOBER	NOVEMBER	DECEMBER

ORGANIZE
your eating habits

WHERE TO START

Food is the first thing that comes to mind when I think about health. As the saying goes, you are what you eat. Eat healthily, and you will be healthy. But wait a minute, is life that simple? I wish it were. However, there are some systems you can implement to put yourself on a better track.

If your goal is to eat healthier meals and serve your family healthy options, that means no more fast food or "cereal for dinner" nights. Instead, I will guide you through planning your meals, so you can always easily and quickly make healthy food and eliminate the need to hit the drive-through for burgers and fries.

Before you start meal planning, I would like to draw your attention to another important topic: creating a "green" kitchen. Think about ways you

could help the environment right now, from your kitchen. After all, a healthy environment and a healthy lifestyle are interwoven.

Try to choose foods that are not wrapped in lots of plastic. Buy things in bulk to save on packaging supplies. Choose organic and minimally processed food as much as you can. Shop from local farmers and opt for foods that are in season. If we all make small changes to our lifestyle, we can significantly improve the environment.

It is time to start planning meals, creating a grocery list, and implementing other steps to get your family on the path to better eating. With consistency and discipline, these will all become part of your daily life.

DEFINE YOUR GOALS

Before we start meal planning, it is important to take the time to think about your goals. What does healthy eating mean to you?

You could be looking for ways to improve your body image or make more purposeful decisions regarding what to buy and what kind of food to eat. Perhaps you have a health condition that you need to be more aware of. It doesn't matter your goal; I believe you can do anything as long as you put your mind to it. You just need to believe in yourself.

Some people like to begin their fitness journey by becoming more mindful of their eating and later start tracking their workout routine. If you think that is the route for you, pay close attention to what you eat and when. You might start to see some patterns. Ask yourself if you are really hungry or if food is a way to deal with emotions, pass the time, or even procrastinate.

Ok, you ate! How do you feel emotionally and physically after that meal or snack? Do you feel good, satisfied, happy, and energized — or do you feel guilty about your choice? Spend a day or a week recording your experiences with food. You might want to log your meals and snacks in a food journal to track that information. You can use a paper or digital tracker to help with this task.

On the other hand, you might feel that a food journal is not for you. I understand how you feel. If that is your case, use this time to write down your intentions for eating healthy and your goals for the coming week and the weeks to come.

FOOD JOURNAL

Breakfast

Lunch

Dinner

Snacks

Water Intake ○ ○ ○ ○ ○

Breakfast

Lunch

Dinner

Snacks

Water Intake ○ ○ ○ ○ ○

Breakfast

Lunch

Dinner

Snacks

Water Intake ○ ○ ○ ○ ○

Breakfast

Lunch

Dinner

Snacks

Water Intake ○ ○ ○ ○ ○

Breakfast

Lunch

Dinner

Snacks

Water Intake ○ ○ ○ ○ ○

Breakfast

Lunch

Dinner

Snacks

Water Intake ○ ○ ○ ○ ○

Breakfast

Lunch

Dinner

Snacks

Water Intake ○ ○ ○ ○ ○

My Intentions for Healthy Eating:

MEAL PLANNING

Meal Planning is easier and less complicated than many think, but it is not a one-size-fits-all system. My step-by-step process will enable you to create a meal plan customized to your family that fits your lifestyle and routine.

As you create your meal plan, you will focus on what is most important to you. Your plan will ensure you meet your most important goals first.

You can follow this simple process to create new plans each week or use it once to create a meal plan you use over and over again (until you decide it's time to change it up!).

Meal planning will help you put your healthy eating goals into action, whether that means changing your diet, being more intentional when shopping, or reinforcing good habits.

Meal planning will also help you save time and money in the kitchen. Here are some tips for effective meal planning:

- Create a list of your favorite meals of the season and refer to it every time you meal plan.

- Set aside one or two hours during the week to prep your food ahead of time. Take the schedule you have created and block out time to shop and prep your meals. You can even set reminders on your online calendar to remember this new routine.

- Try shopping once a week. Fewer trips to the grocery store mean fewer impulse purchases. Stay on budget by planning meals around coupons and sales. It's crucial that your meal planning fits your lifestyle and schedule. When you have a hectic night — perhaps you or your spouse will be traveling or working late, or your kids have sports practice— plan a simple dinner, such as something you can put in the slow cooker. Save the elaborate meals for those days you have time to spare

FAMILY FAVORITES

Make a list of your family's favorite food for quick reference. This list will help you decide what to make when you don't have much time to search for new recipes.

RECIPE	SOURCE

CHECK FOR SUPPLIES

Now is the time when all the work you put into organizing your kitchen will pay off. Check your fridge, freezer, and pantry to see what you already have and make a list of the foods you will need to buy. Getting in the habit of following this step will help you minimize the chances of over-buying supplies, and wasting food and money.

With a list in hand, think about how many times you plan to go to the grocery store per month. Will you buy in bulk? Will you purchase weekly groceries? What will you cook this week? Is a trip to the grocery store necessary? Make a shopping list that is compatible with your goals.

You don't want to overbuy, but you certainly don't want to buy less than you will need either. How often have you forgotten to buy the ingredients for the planned meals? I have done that, and it is not fun. Make sure to write down the ingredients and double-check the recipes for what you might need.

SHOPPING LIST (TEMPLATE)

FRUITS AND VEGETABLES	DAIRY AND EGGS	MEAT AND POULTRY

SEAFOOD	PANTRY STAPLES	BREAD AND GRAINS

BEVERAGES	SNACKS AND SWEETS	HOUSEHOLD ITEMS

GET INSPIRED

We all need inspiration! Most of the recipes we cook on a daily basis are recipes that we know by heart or learned from our elders. Others are found online, in cookbooks, or in magazines. Of course, we frequently put our own spin on the recipes. Sometimes we hide vegetables in the mac and cheese. Sometimes we substitute one ingredient for another in the fridge or change the seasoning. And sometimes we can get tired of eating the same food over and over again. When we get in a routine, we lose the motivation to cook and need to be inspired again.

Finding ways to be inspired to cook is much easier when you know where to look for inspiration and are not afraid of trying new things. I understand the frustration of cooking a new recipe, just to find out the kids won't eat it. That is not to mention the frustration of coming up with something else at the last minute so the kids don't starve. So here are some ideas you could try:

- Cook ingredients you and your family love in a different way;

- Sign up for a local farm delivery. Most of the time, you don't know what you will receive that week, and you will feel like you are in an episode of Chopped;

- Add a new twist to your regular recipes.

Spend some time looking through your cookbooks and magazines for new recipes. You could also check Pinterest, social media, and other great websites for inspiration. To simplify the process, you can keep making those recipes you know your family loves and slowly add new recipes to your repertoire.

You can create a Google doc to save your selected recipes if you are looking for meal inspiration online. When using Pinterest, simply create a new board with the recipes you picked. Use our model to track the options you chose.

RECIPES TO TRY

RECIPE	SOURCE

THE MANY WAYS TO MEAL PLAN

You probably understand this by now, but here is a quick reminder: what works for your best friend might not work for you. This holds true for meal planning as well.

I have tried many ways of meal planning, and I have been doing this for a long time. I remember growing up, my father had a small budget for groceries. My mom never dealt with money very wisely. Sorry Mom, but this is true! That situation led me to start budgeting and meal planning very early in my life, before I even knew there were words for such things. Anyway, I will share two meal-planning methods that I like and work for most people.

First, we will start with the one cuisine per night system. Pick one cuisine per night. Let's say that on Sundays you will have Italian food. On the first Sunday of the month, you could have Spaghetti Carbonara. The second Sunday, you would have stuffed shells. On the third Sunday, Sausage rigatoni. On the fourth Sunday, Fettuccine Alfredo. Even though you have planned four pasta meals, they will be spaced out, and they are different recipes.

The next step is to pick the other cuisines you want to incorporate into your dinners. Some very popular options in our house are Mexican, Italian, American, Asian, and Brazilian. We also plan for one or two nights of leftovers for our busy nights.

The second option for meal planning would be creating one monthly meal plan per season. You will make four main plans that you will rotate throughout the year. Let's say it is wintertime, and just one night a month, you have chili for dinner. If you use this same plan for the whole season, you will only have chili three times.

Meal planning is a crucial part of eating a healthy diet, and there are many benefits linked to it. Take some time to create a plan that works for your family and your lifestyle.

WEEKLY MEAL PLANNING

Breakfast

Snacks

Lunch

Snacks

Dinner

Breakfast

Snacks

Lunch

Snacks

Dinner

Breakfast

Snacks

Lunch

Snacks

Dinner

Breakfast

Snacks

Lunch

Snacks

Dinner

Breakfast

Snacks

Lunch

Snacks

Dinner

Breakfast

Snacks

Lunch

Snacks

Dinner

Breakfast

Snacks

Lunch

Snacks

Dinner

SEASONAL MEAL PLANNER (BREAKFAST)

SUN	MON	TUE	WED	THU	FRI	SAT

SEASONAL MEAL PLANNER (LUNCH)

SUN	MON	TUE	WED	THU	FRI	SAT

SEASONAL MEAL PLANNER (DINNER)

SUN	MON	TUE	WED	THU	FRI	SAT

ORGANIZE YOUR MENU PLAN

After you write down your meal plan:

- Keep it accessible and visible.

- Attach it to your command center or the side of the fridge.

- Don't overcomplicate the process, and there is no need for DIY menu boards, binders, etc.

- Keep it simple!

Meal planning can be as easy or complicated as you make it. You can simply write down dinner options for the week on a sheet of paper or use a color-coded calendar system. You can make 5-star gourmet meals every night, or you can make something as simple as sandwiches. Our goal is to create a menu plan system that works for you.

Make meal planning a habit! Add meal planning to your weekly routine. Each evening before bed, check what is on the schedule for the next night's dinner. That way, you have time to defrost frozen ingredients and ensure you have everything you need.

Remember that there is no right or wrong way to meal plan. If you start out with one menu planning system and find it is not working, try something else. Or, if you find that your menu planning is stressing you out more than it is helpful, take a step back and figure out why. What works for one person might not work for another. It is all about creating a menu plan system that makes your life easier.

ORGANIZE *your health*

IT'S TIME TO GET MOVING

Wait! Before you start moving your body, beginning any new workouts, or doing any exercise at all, you should see your doctor. If you haven't had a check-up in a while, call your doctor's office now to schedule one.

Afterward, your next step is brainstorming your version of a healthy body. What does that mean to you? More flexibility? Greater endurance? The ability to run a marathon?
Identifying your goals will help you be more prepared and empowered to take action when the time comes to get your body moving.

Take a look at how you are treating yourself and your body. Our physical, spiritual, emotional health and physical space are connected. Do you treat your body in a way that shows you love and care for yourself? Would you feed your kids the same food you have been eating? Do you encourage those around you to live a healthy lifestyle?

Take an honest look at your health. What are you proud of? Is there room for improvement? Be honest with yourself so that you can achieve your goals.
I will not tell you how you should look, or share an ideal body image, or how much you should weigh, etc. You will envision your version of a healthy body. How you feel comfortable, healthy, pretty and happy is up to you.

Committing to a seven-day exercise routine can be overwhelming, especially if it has been long since you worked out. Remember that everything is connected: improving our physical health improves our mental health.

Maybe your goal is to become healthy and fit; perhaps you have to gain some weight, or you just want to keep your body active. Perhaps your goal is to run a 5k or a marathon. Whatever your goal is, go for it. Get your support team to cheer on you and live your best life.

HEALTH REALITY CHECK

Brainstorm your version of a healthy body. What does that mean to you? How would you feel and look if you were at your healthiest?

- [ ] _____
- [ ] _____
- [ ] _____
- [ ] _____
- [ ] _____
- [ ] _____
- [ ] _____
- [ ] _____
- [ ] _____
- [ ] _____
- [ ] _____
- [ ] _____
- [ ] _____
- [ ] _____
- [ ] _____
- [ ] _____

CHANGE YOUR HABITS

Make a commitment to yourself to improve your health over the next year. Would you break a promise or a commitment with your best friend? Take this commitment to yourself just as seriously. Set your goals and make a detailed list of the steps you need to follow to reach your goals and make it happen.

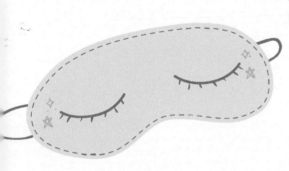

If you are not ready to start an ambitious exercise program, you can at least eliminate bad habits. Here are some examples of bad habits you might have and don't even realize.

- Eating past 8 p.m. or overeating

- Not getting enough sleep

- Not drinking enough water

- Not making self-care a priority

Of course, you are the best person to identify and change your bad habits. The best way to eliminate bad habits is to swap them for better ones. Below are some examples you could follow.

You could tweak your routines and schedule to fix the bad habit of overeating or eating past 8 p.m.. Do the math of how many calories you should eat daily to achieve your goal. If you get cravings at night, sip herbal tea or keep your hands busy with a craft.

It would help if you rejiggered your schedule to fix the lack of sleep. What time do you need to be at work? How much time do you need for your morning routine? Do you go to the gym in the morning? Do you need to drop the kids off at school? Work backward to figure out when you need to wake up. How much sleep does your body need to wake up feeling strong? With those numbers in mind, you will get to an ideal time for when you need to go to sleep. If you have problems getting to bed at night, set alarms for yourself that remind you it's time to start getting ready for sleep.

Not drinking enough water is a problem that many people have. Including me! The way I fixed that was by getting a 750ml reusable water bottle. My goal is to have at least three full bottles a day. I carry my water bottle everywhere with me. I have to drink one full bottle in the morning, one in the afternoon, and one in the evening. Sometimes, when I see that it's almost time to refill my water bottle and I still have water in it, I hurry to finish it up.

Women, especially moms, often prioritize their family members and work responsibilities over their self-care. Not taking care of yourself can start feeling normal. If you haven't put into action the previous exercises of the Organize Yourself Healthy method, please go back to those and think about yourself. Make time to take care of yourself. Your health is a priority.

Substituting one new good habit for a bad habit will take you halfway to your goals. If you notice about ten bad habits you want to change, don't try to change them all at once. Change one to three habits at a time so you don't get overwhelmed. Let new habits become a routine, and then add new ones.

What are the three habits you will start working on right now?

HEALTHY HABITS TRACKER

"SUCCESS COMES FROM WHAT YOU DO CONSISTENTLY!"

HABIT	DAY
	○○○○○○○○○○○○○○ ○○○○○○○○○○○○○○○ ○○○○○○○○
	○○○○○○○○○○○○○○ ○○○○○○○○○○○○○○○ ○○○○○○○○
	○○○○○○○○○○○○○○○ ○○○○○○○○○○○○○○○ ○○○○○○○○○
	○○○○○○○○○○○○○○○ ○○○○○○○○○○○○○○○ ○○○○○○○○○
	○○○○○○○○○○○○○○○ ○○○○○○○○○○○○○○○ ○○○○○○○○○
	○○○○○○○○○○○○○○○ ○○○○○○○○○○○○○○○ ○○○○○○○○○

EXERCISE

I could go on and on about why working out is so important. You might even know these reasons yourself, but I want to remind you about the importance of daily workouts.

Working out reduces stress, lifts your mood, boosts productivity, gives you confidence, builds your self-esteem, helps with self-control, and much more.

What are the exercises you like? Do you enjoy lifting? Cardio? Yoga? Maybe you get bored easily, and Zumba would be a good fit for you? How about jogging? There are many ways to keep your body active. Make a list of 1-5 exercises you would like to try. Number one should be the exercise you enjoy the most, and five should be the least enjoyable.

After you better understand what kind of exercise will get you motivated, it is time to decide when and how often you will exercise.

Your goal should be specific. For example, say: I will exercise on Mondays, Wednesdays, and Fridays for 45 minutes, from 6 to 6:45 in the morning. Or, I will exercise Mondays through Fridays for 30 minutes, from 6:15 to 6:45 in the morning. Write the times you choose in your calendar.

If you currently don't exercise at all, don't say you will start working out every day. You will feel like you are letting yourself down when you miss a workout. Set realistic goals. Reach that goal and then set a bigger goal. It is okay to start simple and get fancier later.

You already know the types of exercises you enjoy, when and how often you will exercise. Now it is time to decide where you will be working out. Will you join the closest gym to your house or work? Does the gym offer child care? What time are the classes you like? Will you join a local moms' fitness group? Will you work with a personal trainer? Will you exercise at home? As you can see, the options are endless.

Schedule your workouts, and treat exercise time like any other appointment. At this point, go back to your schedule and make the proper adjustments to fit your workouts in it. When blocking the time, take into consideration driving time and traffic, then add about 15 minutes for unexpected obstacles that might arise.

WORKOUT TRACKER

"HUSTLE FOR THAT MUSCLE"

	J	F	M	A	M	J	J	A	S	O	N	D
1												
2												
3												
4												
5												
6												
7												
8												
9												
10												
11												
12												
13												
14												
15												
16												
17												
18												
19												
20												
21												
22												
23												
24												
25												
26												
27												
28												
29												
30												
31												

KEYS

- [ ] --
- [ ] --
- [ ] --
- [ ] --
- [ ] --
- [ ] --
- [ ] --
- [ ] --
- [ ] --

DAILY PLANNER (TEMPLATE)

DATE

TOP 3 PRIORITIES

....

....

....

TO-DO LIST

- ○
- ○
- ○
- ○

HOUSEWORK	SELFCARE
GETTING SOCIAL	WORKOUT

MEAL PLAN

BREAKFAST	
LUNCH	
DINNER	
SNACKS	

AFFIRMATIONS

- ○
- ○
- ○
- ○

TODAY'S SCHEDULE

5 AM	
6 AM	
7 AM	
8 AM	
9 AM	
10 AM	
11 AM	
12 AM	
1 PM	
2 PM	
3 PM	
4 PM	
5 PM	
6 PM	
7 PM	
8 PM	
9 PM	
10 PM	
11 PM	
12 AM	

AVOID SELF SABOTAGE

Although the Organize Yourself Healthy lessons are coming to an end, the process of improving ourselves continues. Life happens, routines change, and it will be necessary to adjust your schedule to fit your priorities and lifestyle from time to time. You will need to revisit your plans occasionally, and I want you to know that it is okay.

When life gets overwhelming, take a step back and review the first exercises on organizing your mind and time. If Plan A doesn't work, try Plan B. Achieving your health goals is not easy. It takes a lot of dedication, motivation and self-control. Keep working on your routines, discover what makes you happy and create the life of your dreams. Start each day with what motivates you. End every day feeling like you were in control of your life and did all you could to move in the direction you wanted.

If negative thoughts pop up, take a short walk. When you get tired, find a little bit of energy and motivation to keep moving, exercising, and taking care of yourself. Remind yourself of your purpose every time you are tempted to self-sabotage.

Keep your body and mind active and healthy, and watch your confidence levels rise.

I hope you are as proud of yourself as much as I am proud of you. You took the time to work on your dreams, which is a remarkable achievement.

Take the time to celebrate your victory. You have laid the groundwork to become a healthier, happier person. You are on the path to creating the healthier lifestyle you deserve.

It is incredible to think of what you have accomplished through implementing the Organize Yourself Healthy method:

- You have set clear goals for yourself and mapped out a strategy to achieve them.

- You have created a schedule that ensures you have time to care for your body and soul.

- You have organized your home, making cooking healthy meals and exercising regularly easier.

- You have created a plan to spend consistent and meaningful time with family and friends and built a support system to help you stick to your healthy lifestyle.

- You have devised meal plans to keep you and your family eating well and avoid the dreaded drive-thru.

- You have organized your workout routine to commit to a realistic exercise schedule.

It is time to celebrate your victories and enjoy your healthier, more organized lifestyle. Notice how good your body feels when you take care of yourself. Savor this feeling of accomplishment. You have committed to your physical and mental health. You are treating yourself as you deserve to be treated — with love.

THANK YOU!

As we reach the end of your lifestyle reset with the Organize Yourself Healthy method, I want to extend my deepest gratitude to you. Thank you for entrusting me with your time and commitment to this journey. I hope every page has inspired you, encouraging you toward a life of intention, balance, and fulfillment.

When I started writing this book, my vision was clear—to witness busy moms like you intentionally utilizing their time, resources, routines, personal time, and more, just as I have, to grow into better versions of themselves.

My journey of creating an organized lifestyle and the needs of my home-organizing clients inspired the creation of this book. I sincerely hope that it has served as a motivation for positive change in your life, as well. Organize Yourself Healthy method is different from other methods in many ways. One way that is different is that I intend to update and improve it as needed. I need your help with this. Please email us if you find a typo or think of a way to improve the method or the accountability services linked to the method.

Now, I invite you to join our community and share your accomplishments, your inspirations, and the moments when you became your own source of motivation. Connect with me through social media (@diisorganized) and email (hello@diisorganized.com), and keep me posted on your journey. Your story is an integral part of this collective narrative.

With sincere gratitude and enthusiasm for the thrilling adventure awaiting you,

 www.diisorganized.com

 @diisorganized

 @diisorganized

Made in the USA
Monee, IL
14 January 2024

51783011R00055